BUG BUZZ!

Wayne Gerdtz

OXFORD

UNIVERSITY PRESS

OXFORD
UNIVERSITY PRESS

Great Clarendon Street, Oxford, OX2 6DP, United Kingdom

Oxford University Press is a department of the University
of Oxford. It furthers the University's objective of excellence
in research, scholarship, and education by publishing
worldwide. Oxford is a registered trade mark of Oxford
University Press in the UK and in certain other countries

Text © Wayne Gerdtz 2014

The moral rights of the author have been asserted

First published 2014

British Library Cataloguing in Publication Data
Data available

ISBN: 978-0-19-830802-7

14

Paper used in the production of this book is a natural, recyclable product
made from wood grown in sustainable forests. The manufacturing process
conforms to the environmental regulations of the country of origin.

Printed in Hong Kong by Paramount

Acknowledgements

Series Editor: Nikki Gamble
Cover photo: Tomatito/Shutterstock

Illustrations by Cat MacInnes
Designed and typeset by Cristina Neri, Canary Graphic Design

The publishers would like to thank the following for the permission
to reproduce photographs: **p2/3**: Ian McKinnell/Getty Images; **p4/5
background**: Hiroshi Higuchi/Getty Images; **p4l**: Stephen Dalton/Minden
Pictures/Corbis; **p4r**: Roland Bogush/Getty Images; **p5**: Peter Waters/
Shutterstock; **p6**: Ed Reschke/Getty Images; **p7**: Walter Myers/Science
Photo Library; **p8l**: Danita Delimont/Getty Images; **p8r**: Ian McKinnell/
Getty images; **p9bl**: TeguhSantosa/Getty Images; **p9r**: Jan Stromme/
Getty Images; **p9tl**: Minden Pictures/Masterfile; **p10l**: Papilio/Alamy;
p10r: Marvin Dembinsky Photo Associates/Alamy; **p11bl**: Don Johnston/
Alamy; **p11br**: Thomas Kitchin & Victoria Hurst/First Light/Corbis;
p11tl: Sinclair Stammers/Science Photo Library; **p11tr/23**: Rechtsanwalt/
Shutterstock; **p12**: lauriek/Getty Images; **p13**: Fuse/Getty Images; **p14**:
Berndt Fischer/Getty Images; **p14/15**: Narinbg/Shutterstock; **p15**: F1online
digitale Bildagentur GmbH/Alamy; **p16**: Cisca Castelijns/ Foto Natura/
Minden Pictures/Corbis; **p17**: Leena Robinson/Shutterstock; **p18/19**: Scott
Camazine/Alamy; **p18l**: blickwinkel/Alamy; **p19r**: Stephen Dalton/Minden
Pictures/Corbis; **p19t**: Michael Durham/Minden Pictures/Corbis; **p20**: Ingo
Arndt/Nature Picture Library; **p21b**: Piotr Naskrecki/Minden Pictures/
FLPA; **p21t**: karthik photography/Getty Images; **p22l**: Rolf Nussbaumer
Photography/Alamy; **p22r**: blickwinkel/Alamy; **p23b**: Graphic Science/
Alamy; **p23t**: StudioSmart/Shutterstock

CONTENTS

FIND AN INSECT

Insects are everywhere – there are more insects than any other type of animal on Earth!

Some insects crawl or jump. Some insects fly.

All insects have:

one pair of antennae

a body that has three parts

six legs

a hard outer shell, called an exoskeleton

If you find an animal with all these body parts, you have found an insect!

INSECTS FROM LONG AGO

Insects have lived on Earth for a long time. Many insects were around even before the dinosaurs!

This insect **fossil** is more than 40 million years old!

Millions of years ago, forests buzzed with insects. Some of them were *enormous*. Imagine a dragonfly as big as a duck!

INSECT HOMES

Insects live in many different places. Just like humans, they build their homes in places where they can find food.

hot deserts

lakes and rivers

snow-topped mountains

your home

rainforests

In rainforests, scientists think there are millions of types of insects that nobody has ever seen!

9

BABY INSECTS

baby cockroach

All baby insects hatch from eggs.

Some baby insects look like little adult insects, such as these baby cockroaches.

Other baby insects look completely different from the adults. They go through big changes as they grow up.

1 A butterfly starts life as a caterpillar in a small egg.

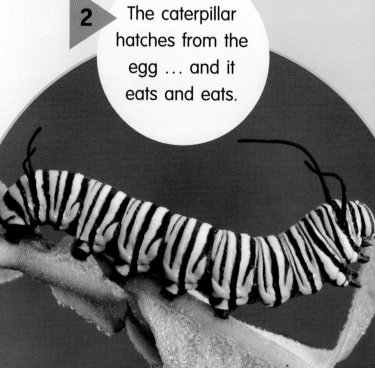

2 The caterpillar hatches from the egg … and it eats and eats.

adult cockroach

4 ... into a butterfly.

3 The caterpillar becomes a chrysalis (*say* kris-a-lis) and starts changing ...

SPECIAL EYES

Many insects have special eyes called compound eyes. Compound eyes are made up of many tiny parts – these are like lots of mini eyes.

Some insects have compound eyes that help them look at different things all at once. This means that insects can find food *and* look out for danger at the same time!

tiny parts

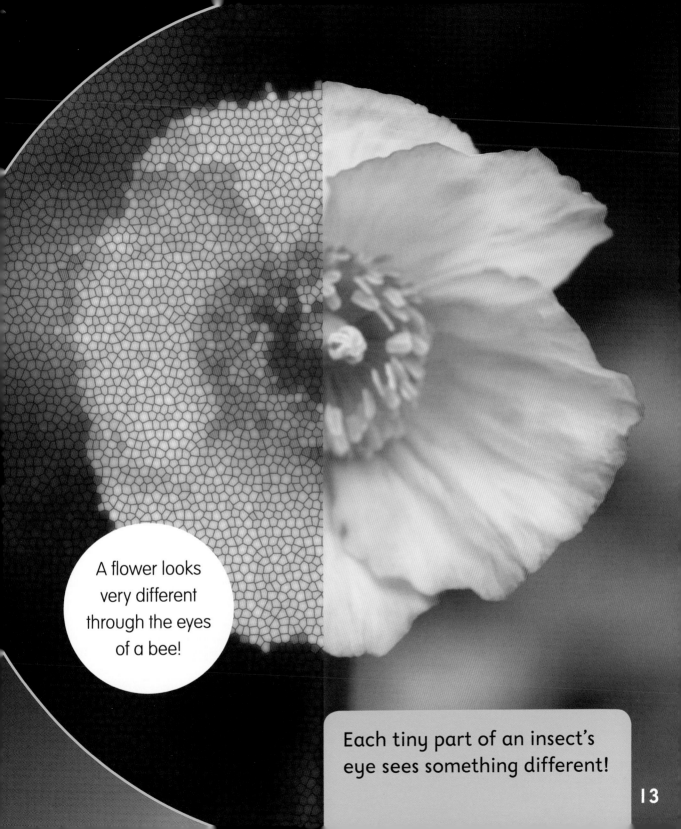

A flower looks very different through the eyes of a bee!

Each tiny part of an insect's eye sees something different!

AMAZING MOUTHS

Insects don't have teeth! Instead, their mouths have special parts to help them eat. Each type of insect has different parts in its mouth, depending on the food it eats.

Mulberry borers chew wood.

Some insects have mouths that bite and chew.

Shield bugs suck juices from plants.

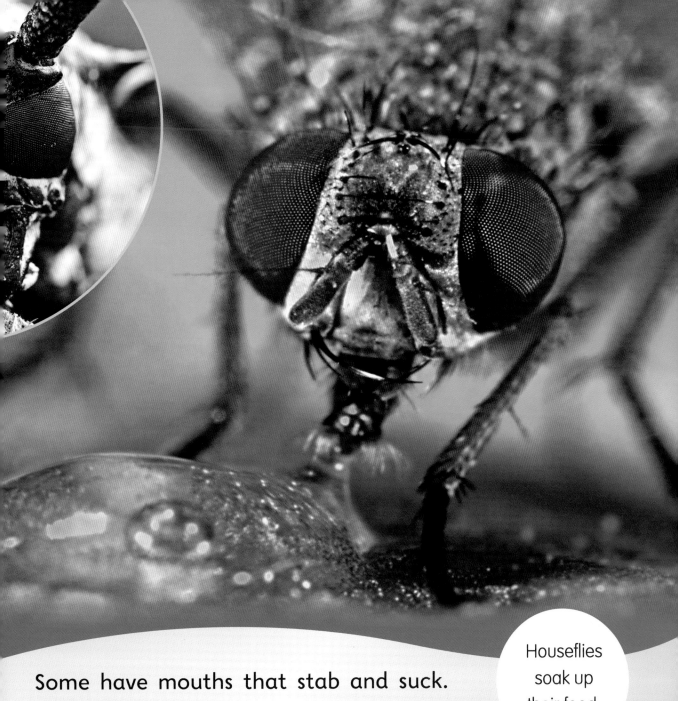

Houseflies soak up their food.

Some have mouths that stab and suck.

Other insects have mouths that soak up food, just like a sponge!

WONDERFUL WINGS

Insects were the first flying animals on Earth. Most insects have four wings. Other insects, such as flies, only have two wings.

A dragonfly's wings are so thin that they are see-through.

Dragonflies have four long wings. This means they can fly very fast.

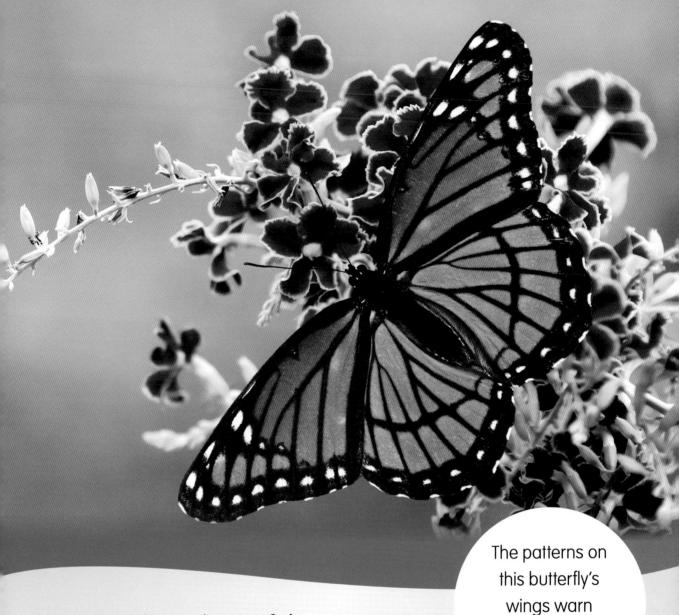

The patterns on this butterfly's wings warn predators that it tastes bad!

Butterflies have beautiful patterns on their wings. Sometimes these patterns help to protect the butterfly from **predators**. The patterns also help to **attract** other butterflies.

SIX SUPER LEGS

Insects have six legs and each leg has six main parts. Insects use their legs to do different jobs such as burrowing, catching food, jumping and swimming.

Mole crickets use their strong front legs to dig.

The praying mantis has legs like hooks to hold its food.

Grasshoppers use their long legs to jump away from predators.

Backswimmers have legs like paddles so they can swim across the water on their backs.

If a young stick insect loses a leg, it can grow a new one!

19

WEIRD AND WONDERFUL

There are lots of weird and wonderful insects all around the world.

Puss moth caterpillars make faces at predators to scare them away.

Treehoppers use their long, spiky horns to scare away predators.

The gladiator insect gets its name from its exoskeleton, which looks like **armour**.

WE NEED INSECTS

Even though some insects bite or sting, insects can also be very helpful.

Insects such as bees, wasps and butterflies move pollen from flower to flower. This helps plants to grow new fruit and seeds for us to eat.

Baby insects, such as grubs, eat our food scraps.

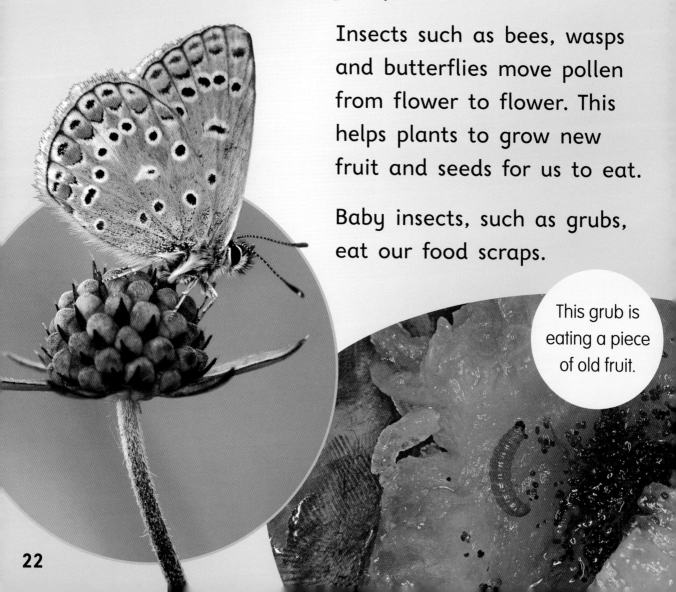

This grub is eating a piece of old fruit.

Some insects make food
that people like to eat —
honey is made by bees!

Some insects, such as
ladybirds, eat pests that
damage our plants.

So next time you tell an
insect to buzz off, remember:
we need insects!

GLOSSARY

armour: a tough outer layer to protect a soft body, such as metal armour worn in battle

attract: to draw attention

chrysalis: the hard outer shell on a moth or butterfly in the stage before it becomes an adult with wings

fossil: the hard remains of an animal or plant that lived millions of years ago

predators: animals that hunt and eat other animals

INDEX